DURHAM PEOPLE

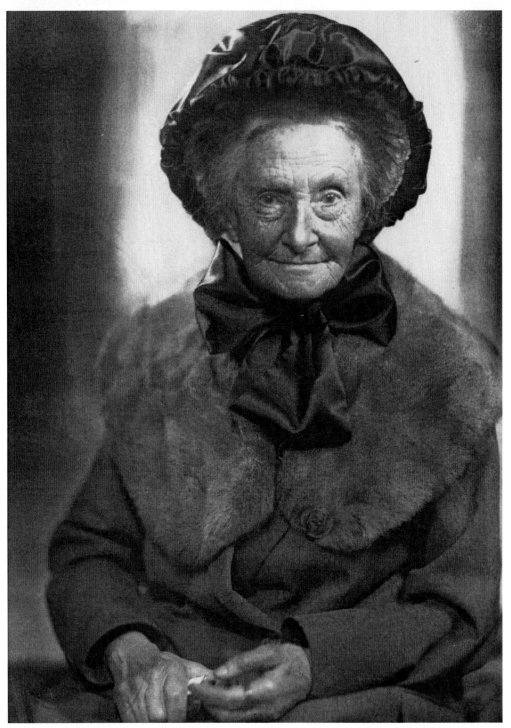

An exhibition photograph featuring an old lady, taken by Daisy Spence (*née* Edis), the famous Durham photographer. She took over the business from her father John Reed Edis who first started in the 1890s in Gilesgate, moving to Saddler Street in 1899. Daisy's work was of a very high standard. She specialized in portraits and exhibited overseas as far away as the USA and Japan. Daisy died in 1964 and is buried in St Giles' Churchyard.

DURHAM PEOPLE

MICHAEL RICHARDSON

This book was first published in 1994 by Sutton Publishing

Reprinted with revisions in 2009 by
The History Press
The Mill, Brimscombe Port,
Stroud, Gloucestershire, GL5 2QG
www.thehistorypress.co.uk

ISBN 978 0 7509 0708 8

Cover pictures:
Front: Hayton's Novelty Bazaar, Durham Indoor Market, *c.* 1909.
Back: Sherburn Road Ends, *c.* 1904.

Typesetting and origination by
Sutton Publishing.
Printed and bound in Great Britain by Marston Book Services Limited, Oxford.

Contents

George E. Summerscales, 1910. In the annals of Durham City Rugby Club the name of George Summerscales will be inscribed among the greatest. 'Summer' played his first game in 1896 at the age of seventeen. He made no fewer than fifty-one appearances in County Championship matches. Among his trophies was an international cap against the first All Blacks in 1905. The honour he prized most was when he skippered City to victory in the 1910 cup final against Hartlepool Rovers at Ashbrooke, their first success for twenty-two years.

Introduction

Durham is an enchanting city. In the words of Sir Nikolaus Pevsner, it is 'one of the great experiences of Europe. The group of cathedral, castle and monastery on the rock can only be compared to Avignon and Prague.' The peninsula with its high promontory is beautifully wooded and almost surrounded by the River Wear as it meanders to Sunderland and the North Sea; it is a memorable sight. Much of the charm of the city itself remains with its byways, despite the new road which tore the heart out of it in the 1960s.

Durham is of course an historic city. Where else is there a Romanesque cathedral built within the bailey of a Norman castle? In 1993, Durham Cathedral celebrated the 900th anniversary of its foundation, but a church had stood on the site since 995 when the monks had settled there to build a shrine for St Cuthbert, whose body they had brought from Lindisfarne more than a hundred years before to escape the Vikings. That settlement gave rise to a town, the millennium of which fell in 1995. Little wonder that the complex of the cathedral and the castle was declared a World Heritage site in 1987. The continuation of the spiritual and temporal side by side symbolizes the peculiar history of the area. In the Middle Ages the bishops had ruled the County Palatine like princes.

This collection of two hundred photographs and sketches, drawn from the archive developed by Michael Richardson in recent years, concentrates on the people rather than the place. The vast majority of the photographs have never been published before, and many local families are represented in the group and individual portraits.

Coal, mined in the region from Roman times, constituted the very life-blood of the county in the nineteenth and early twentieth centuries, and heavy industry dominated the region (but not the city) until Palmer's ironworks and shipyards closed in 1934, the prelude to the famous Jarrow March of 1936. The photograph of three young boys following their fathers into lives in the pits is for me especially poignant. The industrial production necessitated transport, by road, by sea, and by rail after the north-east pioneered railways in the 1820s. Great physical obstacles were overcome to provide the railway system by the Victorians, and the viaduct in Durham City, built on sand and completed in 1857, is an outstanding example of engineering skills as well as a beautiful object in its own right.

The Miners' Gala held on a Saturday in July, and now only tenuously surviving, was a great event in the city around the turn of the century. As a resident has recorded:

> We always went to see it, watching the proceedings from an upstairs window. During the morning contingents from the surrounding collieries streamed down the big bank from the station, each with its band playing and its huge banner carried by six men – two holding the poles and four the guy ropes. In the afternoon, the miners held their big meeting on the racecourse, and in the evening we watched them coming back up the North Road. But oh what a difference! The banners now lurched all over the road, and no doubt the music also reflected the men's state of mind and body.

Durham City, 20 miles from the coast but with good road and rail links, was a natural centre for military activities. The barracks, now the Vane-Tempest Hall, survive in Gilesgate as a reminder of past prowess, though many Durham men were too small for some regiments and had to join battalions based outside the county – the average height of Durham recruits in 1914 was only 5 ft 4 in. The men of the area were particularly patriotic, though when the 8th Durham Light Infantry marched to the front in April 1915 few could have imagined that one-fifth of their number would be killed within a few days. They had responded to stirring calls from members of the local nobility and clergy.

Durham men and women, as Michael Richardson's photographs demonstrate, played as hard as they worked, gaining an enviable reputation for amateur dramatics and leek growing, celebrating national events and festivals with street parties, maypole dancing or morris dancing, and organizing annual events like the horse parade and the Miners' Gala which attracted attention from far outside the city.

The occupations of the residents of Durham City were on the one hand miners, craftsmen and manual workers, for the expansion of the iron and coal trade had brought a lot of artisans to the county, and on the other hand professionals, churchmen, academics and scholars of the cathedral and university. In between these two categories were the traders and shopkeepers of all kinds who served both. The university remained small until its separation from Newcastle in 1963, but there were the training colleges – Bede from 1838, St Hild's from 1858 and Neville's Cross from 1922 – and as the county town Durham was also an administrative centre. In 1939 the city had an insured population of 18,500; 12 per cent were in coal mining, 14.3 per cent in the distributive trades and 10.9 per cent in professional services. Consequently, Michael Richardson has photographs of people who followed a great range of occupations – chemists and roadworkers, hawkers and horse dealers, coal deputies and coach proprietors. Some of the occupations were rural, for Durham remains a small city and the countryside is not far away. For centuries the countryside extended on the south to the very foot of the cathedral. As in rural districts, most working-class families kept a pig to supplement their diet, and as late as the 1950s Durham was famous for its horse fairs.

Hilda Wilson Davison, who was a regular visitor to her grandparents in the city in the early 1900s, has written in a private memoir: 'I don't remember ever seeing a motor vehicle in those early days; all the traffic was horse-drawn. Private buses from the main hotels used to go up to the station to meet the trains; and the 'Black Maria' was a common sight, carrying prisoners from the station to the Gaol. It was a black van with a little barred window high up on one side, and at the back a policeman sat on a small seat outside the vehicle.' Michael Richardson has a photograph of the van in this collection.

The coming of the assize judge was another event in the city's calendar. He was conveyed in near regal splendour – an ornate closed carriage drawn by two horses, with wigged coachman on the box and two footmen standing behind. All three men were in elaborate uniforms, but the soberly dressed judge must have been a disappointment to onlookers! When the assizes were about to begin, two trumpeters would blow a fanfare outside the court. People believed that the fanfare was saying: 'He that is clear, Need not fear, For the judge is near.'

The city and its residents experienced poverty as well as prosperity. The worst year of the slump was in fact 1932 when two in every five of County Durham's insured population were unemployed. Indeed, unemployment in the north-east remained persistently higher than the national average, and local wages to this day are generally lower than in other parts of the kingdom. The bleakness of some of the urban scenes, as in a picture of Gilesgate Moor in the collection, symbolizes the low standard of living which prevailed even in fairly recent times. The slum clearance policy of the local council in the 1930s was too little too late, and there is independent testimony to the harshness of conditions in the city before and immediately after the Second World War.

Durham people are a resilient group, rightly proud of their traditions, and this book is a tribute to them and to the special ethos of the district.

Section One
MEET THE PEOPLE

Mrs Sally Savage from 27 Sherburn Road, early 1950s. This view is taken at the family allotment. It was quite common in County Durham for householders to supplement their diet by having a domestic pig. Everything would be used apart from its squeak.

Just a Line to Say:

If you want a first-class Photo or Enlargement of yourself, or from a copy, you can obtain all you require at the Science & Art Photo Co., 69, Saddler Street, Durham. Outdoor Groups a Speciality, and having the largest Studio in the North of England groups can be taken inside in any weather. Prices are as low as possible for good work. You can get Photos from 3s. 6d. per dozen. Any Enquiry will have the personal attention of

Yours truly,

Geo. Fillingham,

Manager.

P.S.—Photos in this Guide taken by the Science & Art Co.

Photo by Science & Art Co.   Durham.

An advertisement for the Science and Art Company, 69 Saddler Street, *c.* 1909, the manager being George Fillingham. Fillingham's still exists today, operating at Elvet Bridge. It was Durham's longest surviving photographery business. It closed in March 2000 after 90 years.

John George Blackburn, cab proprietor, 50 Dragon Villa, Durham, 1890s. Mr Blackburn arranged pleasure parties, school trips, weddings and funerals. He was also a leading local preacher and took great interest in the local Primitive Methodist Church at Dragon Villa.

John Willy Pattinson, *c.* 1910, taken by John Edis. A prominent Salvation Army leader, he owned and ran the Dunelm Café in Old Elvet. In 1927 he was baking 28,000 loaves of bread per month. He was mayor of the city in 1930 and had the honorary freedom of the city conferred on him by the town council in 1950. In St Nicholas' Church a fine stained-glass window showing the Salvation Army crest was erected in 1963 in memory of Alderman Pattinson and his wife.

Golden Wedding photograph of Joseph and Alice Chapelow, May 1927. Joseph had a chemist's shop at 14 Claypath; he was also a photographer. He bottled and sold aerated waters at his shop and his bottles are now very rare. The Chapelows were strongly connected with St Giles' Church. Joseph, who was church warden, was also in the choir for many years. His wife was a long-standing member of the Mothers' Union.

William Henderson, FRHistS, *c.* 1874. William ran Henderson's Carpet Factory with his brother John. He was author of The Folklore of the Northern Counties of England and the Borders, 1866, and Notes and Reminiscences of My Life as an Angler, 1876. He was mayor of the city in 1849 and helped to raise money by public subscription for the building of the new town hall.

The Right Revd Handley Carr Glyn Moule, *c.* 1910, Bishop of Durham 1901–20. From 1898 he was honorary chaplain to Queen Victoria and on her death in 1901 was appointed chaplain-in-ordinary to Edward VII.

Edward Cummings, farrier, cartwright and general smith, 1920s. On the left is Edward Cummings and right is David Young, lamp oil man from the Coach Opening. The Coach Opening stood to the left of the Three Horse Shoes, Gilesgate. The name originated from the Railway Coach, an old public house which had stood on the site before the Three Horse Shoes.

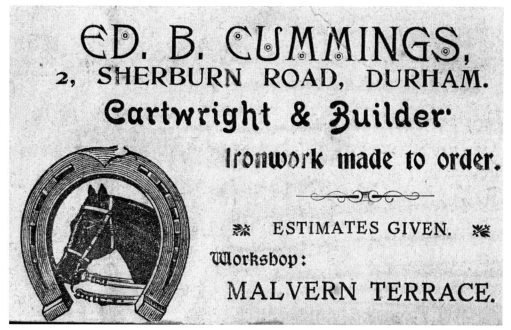

Business card belonging to Edward B. Cummings, 1920s.

Mrs Hopps polishing a copper jug in the Wheatsheaf public house, 3 Claypath, *c.* 1949. Mrs Hopps lived at Old Durham Farm. In the early 1960s Durham lost many old public houses because of the new road system.

Cycle dealer, Benny Clark, 85 Claypath, *c.* 1949. Benny also had a toy stall at Durham Indoor Market. At one time the property was a showroom for Lowes Marble Works and in 1936 an office for the British Union of Fascists (Mosley's Blackshirts). It is now a takeaway pizza shop.

The Savage family from Gilesgate in their Sunday best, 1903. Frederick Thomas (F.T.) Savage was originally from Hallgarth Street where he was a deputy at Elvet Colliery. He had a distinguished army record, having joined the Durham Rifle Volunteers as far back as 1873. He had more than forty years' service with the volunteers and later the Territorial Army. Left to right: Margaret Ethelina, Minnie, Frederick Thomas (father), Richard Ethelbert, Sarah Jane, John, Isabella (mother, née Button), James Edward (the author's grandfather), Alfred Septimus. This was a studio group taken by the Science and Art Company of 69 Saddler Street, Durham.

James Button (the author's great-great-grandfather) in his working clothes as a rail platelayer at Belmont, *c.* 1881. When James lived in Gilesgate in 1861 he was listed as a seaman; in 1871 he was a hawker of earthenware. He later moved to Belmont and lived at Old Station House.

Mary Button, née Burnside, wife of James Button, is seen here, *c.* 1896, with her granddaughter Mary. It is interesting to see the style of the costumes of that period.

Charles William Savage and family (son of F.T. Savage), 1917, 27 Alma Place, Gilesgate Moor. William enlisted in 1898 in the 1st Kings Dragoon Guards. He saw service in South Africa in the Boer War and later in the First World War. He was discharged in August 1915, on account of his wounds. His son William, standing to his right, was killed at Sherburn House Colliery in September 1923 aged sixteen.

Mrs Sarah Jane Savage, (daughter of F.T. Savage) general dealer, 24 Marshall Terrace, Gilesgate Moor, 1972. Mrs Savage started the business just after the Second World War. She ran one of the original open-all-hours shops. She sold almost everything from a pin to a bag of coal. Sarah married her cousin, William Savage.

17

Dean Alington and his wife in retirement in Hertfordshire, *c.* 1953. Dean Alington, dean of Durham 1933–51, was behind the setting up of Alington House Community Centre in the North Bailey and author of many books. In 1943 he founded the Durham City Trust. He had been headmaster of Eton before he became dean. His dog was named Mu after the Mothers' Union.

William Arthur Hall Shepherd, mayor of the city, 1957. He had also been mayor in 1943. He was born at Neville's Cross and was in business as a master tailor. His daughter was mayoress during both terms of office.

John William Blackburn, cab proprietor, 50 Dragon Villa, Sherburn Road, *c.* 1949. John Willy took over his father's business and with his bus, the Dragon Queen, he served the local villages. He was also on the Belmont Parish Council for many years.

Mr George Rolling, fruit and vegetable dealer, 1920s. He later opened a shop on Sunderland Road near Edge Court, Gilesgate. Later still, when business was flourishing, he had a shop built at 45a Sunderland Road, now Alan's Hairdressers. The small hatch at the bottom left-hand corner was where the ash toilets were emptied.

Mr Smith outside his butcher's shop at 88A Claypath, 1899. Open windows were common for butchers and fishmongers in the city until the late 1940s.

Nichol Chilton outside his shop, 26 Sherburn Road, Gilesgate, c. 1914. Nichol was born in Gilesgate. His son Thomas took over the business which lasted until the early 1970s. Donald Crampton, who had a successful business in New Elvet, was a grandson and Ruth Heslop, who had a shop near the Green in Gilesgate, was Nichol's daughter.

The Pattison family in the garden of Ivy Cottage, which stood in the grounds of the Girls' High School near Brown's Boat House, *c.* 1913. It is interesting to see children's toys of the period. Back row, left to right: Joseph William Pattison, Janet Pattison. Middle row: Mary Isobella Pattison, Marjory Hornsby, Margaret Emily Pattison. Front row: Thomas William Pattison and Dorothy Hornsby (the Hornsbys lived at the Drill Hall, Gilesgate).

The Revd H.E. Fox MA, vicar of St Nicholas' Church from 1882 to 1895. Fox succeeded his uncle the Revd George Townsend Fox, vicar from 1856 to 1882. It was his uncle who paid for the erection of the spire at his own expense.

L/Cpl. Richard Savage, 10th Royal Hussars, c. 1917. Richard is seen here with his wife, Annie, who was a maid in Lord Kitchener's household. Richard met Annie while on leave in the south of England. Richard was born in Hallgarth Street, and later moved to Gilesgate as a child. Around 1928, when Richard left the army, he was found a position in the Law Courts in London by an officer whose life he had saved in the First World War.

Section Two

THE HAPPIEST DAYS
OF THEIR LIVES

Albert Richardson (the author's great grandfather), head gardener at St Hild's College, *c.* 1918. Until the 1950s gardening was taught as part of the curriculum. At the college garden show in 1922 Albert exhibited eighteen varieties of potato grown in the college grounds.

St Oswald's National School (infants), Church Street, *c.* 1895. To the right of the teacher is Alfred Septimus Savage. The school had opened in 1845 and cost about £1,500.

St Hild's Model School, Gilesgate, *c.* 1897, opened 30 May 1864. This is one of only three known photographs taken by Joseph Chapelow, chemist, photographer and aerated water manufacturer of 14 Claypath.

A class from St Giles' Church of England School, *c.* 1901. The Revd Francis Thomas, vicar of St Giles, is standing on the far right, to his left, back row, is Alfred Savage and below him, is his brother Richard. The school was known locally as the Gate School. St Giles' Filling Station now occupies the site.

Blue Coat girls, *c.* 1900. The teacher on the left is Miss Morgan and on the right is Mrs Fish, the headmistress. Back row, far right, is Nora Young.

25

A Midsummer Night's Dream performed by Durham Girls' Grammar School, Providence Row, c. 1927. The school is now Durham Sixth Form Centre.

Neville's Cross College, staff and seniors, c. 1929. The college was opened in September 1921. In 1939 it moved to Bede and later to Hatfield for the duration of the war, as the college was taken over by the War Office as a casualty clearing station.

A classroom scene at Blue Coat School, Claypath, around 1914. Front row, fourth from left, is Thomas William Pattison from Ivy Cottage.

Millburngate Nursery, 1951. It was built during the last war. The Millburngate shopping complex now occupies the site.

The staff from Whinney Hill School, *c.* 1957. Back row: Miss Williams, Mrs Fawcett, Mrs Webster, Mrs Palle, Mrs Horner, Miss Lowes and Miss Bramwell. Front row: -?-, Miss Gowland, Mrs Ridley, Miss Richardson, Miss Flemming (headmistress), Miss Barker, Mrs Dawson, Miss Wilkinson and Mrs Robinson. The school was officially opened by Brig. Gen. Sir Conyers Surtees on 15 September 1932. The school closed in July 2009 after 77 years.

Gilesgate Moor Junior Mixed School, Class 1, 1951. Second row from back, seventh from the left if Frank Richardson, the author's father. The school was also known locally as the 'Tin School' because it was constructed with corrugated iron sheets.

Section Three
HIGH DAYS
AND HOLIDAYS

Blue Coat School, Claypath. Morris dancers at the May Day festivals held in the schoolyard, 1963.
The first May Day festival was held in 1933.

Frederick Menspeth Young, *c.* 1910, coachman to the high sheriffs of the county of Durham from 1897 until 1914. Mr Young was a cab driver at Peele's livery stables which stood behind the Royal County Hotel.

Whinney Hill welcomes George V and Queen Mary to the city, 10 October 1928. The first phase of the street was built by the city council in 1926 as part of the slum clearance scheme.

Easter Fair on the Sands, Durham City, c. 1927. The Sands belong to the freemen of the city, and have been the site of fairs of all descriptions for hundreds of years.

Student Rag Week, Palace Green, 1948. Wood & Watson Ltd for many years loaned to the university students wagons and drivers for the carnival parades. The parades faded out in the early 1970s.

The grandstand which stood on the racecourse, seen here on Regatta Day, *c.* 1885. The races dated back as far as 1665 and continued until 1887. In the distance is Whinney Hill.

32

Durham City Horse Parade travelling down Gilesgate Bank, *c.* 1910. The parade started at the barracks (Vane-Tempest Hall) and travelled through the city and then back to the barracks to be judged. This was an annual occasion, which involved many people and businesses in the city and the surrounding villages. The streets were lined with spectators for the show and the horse parade was an event comparable with the Miners' Gala.

Robert Ebdon, landlord of the Brewers Arms, 80 Gilesgate, and, on the right, Thomas Lee, *c.* 1913. They were entrants in the Durham City Horse Parade at the barracks. (Vane Tempest Hall)

George Rolling from the Co-operative Store in Claypath, *c.* 1909. He was an entrant in the horse parade. On his cart is a typical Edwardian bedroom suite complete with washstand.

Mrs Emily Studholme, manageress of the Rex Cinema, Gilesgate Moor. This photograph was taken on her last opening night at the Rex, 24 January 1958. The last film shown was the action-packed Eagle Squadron.

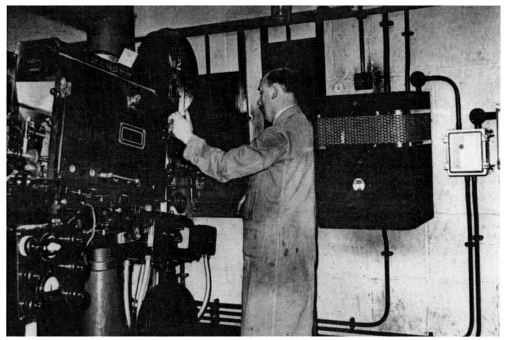

Mr Edgar Denham, projectionist at the Majestic Cinema on Sherburn Road Estate, c. 1952. The Majestic is now a bingo hall.

Visit of Her Royal Highness the Princess Elizabeth, 23 October 1947. The princess is seen here leaving the cathedral on Palace Green. Passes were issued by the town clerk, George Bull, and instructed the holder to hand them to the policeman on duty.

Durham Miners' Gala on the racecourse, c. 1949. The gala was at its peak in the late 1940s, with crowds of up to 200,000. The banner was from Leasingthorne Colliery.

Miners' Gala, 1954, at Old Elvet. Visiting speakers that year were the Rt. Hon. Sir Hartley Shawcross QC, MP, the Rt. Hon. Nye Bevan MP and Bessie Braddock MP. The first Miners' Gala was held at Wharton Park, 12 August 1871. Each July thousands of coalminers and their families would take over the city for the day. The building on the left was the Dunelm Café, now part of the Royal County Hotel. The arched entrance on the left is that of Chapel Passage; this led to the old Methodist Chapel, built in 1808 and demolished in the 1960s.

An aerial view of Old Durham Gardens, *c.* 1949. In the 1920s Old Durham Gardens were a popular weekend attraction. They advertised dancing, a putting-green, a running track, tennis-courts and a tea garden. The Pineapple Inn was attached to the gardens. By 1926 it had lost its licence and thereafter only sold soft drinks. The original Hanging Gardens of Old Durham belonged to the manor house, which was inherited in 1630 by the Heaths of Kepier; the gazebo and walled garden are all that is left of the ancient house. In 1939 Mr Jack Hay from Gilesgate discovered fragments of Roman tiles in the nearby sand quarry. This led to the discovery of a Roman bath house. An archaeological dig was carried out, but sadly the remains were later destroyed by quarrying.

Empire Day at Blue Coat School, *c.* 1949. The first Empire Day was held in 1902. George Savage is in the front row, third from the left, dressed as John Bull, on the right in a Welsh costume is Maureen Metcalfe and to her left is David Larke.

Dancing around the Maypole on May Day in Blue Coat schoolyard, Claypath, *c.* 1963. The white washed cottage in the school yard belonged to the caretaker.

Children from Annand Road, Gilesgate, collecting a penny for the Guy, *c.* 1955. Left to right: Alan Greaves, Peter Hughes, Eddie Jenkins, Victor Richardson, Alan Dickson and Tony Greaves.

Victory in Europe Day, John Street, May 1945. John Street is near the city viaduct, and the railway embankment can be seen at the rear. The lack of men is quite noticeable. It was some time after VE Day before the soldiers were demobbed.

Victory in Europe Party held in Magdalene Street, Gilesgate, May 1945. The relief at the end of hostilities in Europe is evident on the faces of the people, though probably many had lost relatives and friends in the war. Back row fourth from left is Lionel Richardson, the author's grandfather and the boy third from the right in the front row is Frank Richardson, the author's father.

Sledging on the Observatory Field, *c.* 1947. Observatory Field has been a popular sledging spot since Victorian times. The field is now owned by Durham School.

The bandstand at Old Durham Gardens, *c.* 1933. This view was taken from the rear of what was the Pineapple Inn, now a private residence.

Section Four
LEISURE PURSUITS

The Wheatsheaf Leek Club, 1957. The Wheatsheaf stood at the bottom of Claypath and was demolished to make way for the new through road. Fourth from the left is Fred Davis and on the far right is Alf Coyne.

The King William IV, which stood at the bottom of North Road, *c.* 1966. The solid oak front door was salvaged by Mrs Watson of Kepier Farm and is now the main door of the farmhouse. On the left was Lawson's newsagents shop.

The Five Ways Inn, Miss Reece's sweet shop and Stanton's Fish and Chip Shop, 130 Millburngate, *c.* 1966. To the left can be seen the construction of Millburngate Bridge.

The Waterloo Hotel, 61 Old Elvet, *c.* 1964. On the left is the old County Court built in 1871, which in later years became the local food office. They were both demolished in the early 1970s to make way for the New Elvet Road bridge. The building on the far left is now the Swan and Three Signets public house.

The old Three Horse Shoes, 64 Framwellgate. This building was demolished in the early 1960s. On the right of the picture is the original site of the well, known as the Framwell head, which carried water to the pant in Durham Market Place.

Miss Ann and Miss Sarah Palmer (sisters), who ran Palmers Temperance Hotel, 4 North Road, *c.* 1926.

Palmers Temperance Hotel and Café, 4 North Road, *c.* 1900. On the right was the Primitive Methodist Chapel. Now demolished and rebuilt in a simialr style, the ground floor is occupied by Burger King.

The Durham Ox, 39 Gilesgate, *c.* 1933. This public house stood to the left of the Drill Hall at the bottom of Gilesgate Bank. At one time it was known as the Bull and Dog Inn. The public house got its name from the famous Durham Ox which was exhibited throughout England and Scotland in the late eighteenth century. Note the fine granite setts.

The 'Volunteer Arms' Hotel, 47 Gilesgate, *c.* 1935. The landlord was Vincent Tindale, seen here wearing a waistcoat. The hotel stood at the bottom of Gilesgate Bank, above Station Lane.

St Nicholas' Boys' Club, Claypath, seen here on a fishing trip, *c.* 1955, taken by Joe Robinson.

St Nicholas' Church Choir outing. The picture was taken at Blackhall Rocks near Hartlepool on 17 July 1884 by the Revd H.E. Fox, vicar of the church and first chairman of the Durham City Camera Club, which was founded in 1892.

Gilesgate Scouts, *c.* 1947, at Vane-Tempest Hall on 'bob a job' week. The Gilesgate Scouts came into existence in about 1926. The names of some of the people in the group are Billy Pallas, Billy Griffiths, David Coates and Frank Bilton.

The Gilesgate Archery Club, Gilesgate Welfare Association (Vane-Tempest Hall), c. 1947. Left to right: Cyril Walker, Dorothy Cole, Colin McGowan, J.E. Studholme, George Cole, ? Tiplady.

St Nicholas' Church Boys' Brigade, *c.* 1904, seen here in Blue Coat schoolyard, Claypath. The vicar is Mr Bottomley, the man with the beard. It is interesting to note that the boys are carrying rifles. Many lads from the Boys' Brigade were later killed during the First World War. In St Nicholas' Church the First World War memorial records the names of the brigade members who gave up their lives for king and country.

Mrs Alington and the Cathedral Widows in Alington House, *c.* 1951. The Cathedral Widows' origin goes back hundreds of years. Mrs Alington is seen holding flowers.

The Rover steam engine, *c.* 1962, built in 1913 and renovated by Mr George Flynn at his garage at the top of North Road. Fourth from the right is Bill Nichols.

The Criterion, Framwellgate Bridge, c. 1909. The Criterion, or the 'Cri' as it was known, was first established in 1848 by Mr Herbert Robson. In 1894 it was bought by Mr Thomas Colpitts and his cousin Mr T. Burton. The 'Cri' was described as a friendly place where a working man could relax in good company after a hard day's work.

St Nicholas' Church Boys' Club on one of their weekend trips, seen here near Kepier, c. 1955. Photograph taken by Joe Robinson.

Section Five
SPORTING LIFE

Bede Model School rugby team, Gilesgate 1922. The New Bede Model School was built on Bede Bank at the west end of the college site and was opened on 20 February 1886. The Model School closed its doors for the last time in July 1933. The building was renamed Carter House after Miss Phyllis Carter and her father in 1985.

Gilesgate Moor Council School football team, 1921. The young lad in front of the teacher on the right is John Oliver from Gilesgate Moor. The school opened in 1905 and was later renamed Gilesgate Moor Junior Mixed.

Gilesgate Moor Council School football team, 1951. The deputy headmaster was Mr Kirk. Top row, left to right: J. Garfoot, B. Newby, B. Lumley, K. Bryan, B. Mansfield, B. Proctor, -?-. Bottom row: F. Richardson, B. Alderson, J. Bell, J. Lee, D. Ferguson, A. Gravestock.

St Oswald's football team, Elvet, 1914. Many parishes in the city had their own football teams.

Mackay's Carpet Factory football team, *c.* 1949. Back row, left to right: John Mackay, Walter Shea, Tommy Little, Ken Johnson, Wilf Anderson, Tucker Metcalf, Tommy Sharpe, Wilf Helm, Percy Helm. Front row: Harold Buckston, Alan Davies, Gary Marley, Jim Crampton, John Cooper and the mascot, Wilf Anderson's son.

St Leonard's RC School football team, League Cup winners, 1953. The photograph was taken in the school grounds. Top row, left to right: M. O'Brian, M. Doran, R. Crawford, T. Hopper, F. Richardson, C. Davies, T. Kegan. Bottom row: E. Hutchinson, B. Barr, B. Bowes, J. Barret, D. Laing, B. Clark, A. Sutherland. The team strip was green and white.

Mackay's Carpet Factory football team, *c*. 1920. Top row, left to right: -?-, Jackie Walker, Bobby Allenby, Jackie Burnip, Bobby Allison. Middle row: Billy Renwick, John Killian, Bob MacMorran, Jimmy Crampton, Harry Aves. Front row: Jack Smith, Thomas Rowntree, -?-.

Bede College Swimming Club, 1933. Back row, left to right: H.H. Christian, J.E. Brigham, W.E. West, J.W. Martin, A. Wilson. Front row: J.C. Willcox, L.J. Webster, W. Nash, G.S. Webb, L.F. Mills.

Durham Wasps, 1950. The Wasps' origin goes back to 1942 when Canadian airmen were drafted into the area. In the early 1940s Durham had thirty-five Canadian National Hockey League Stars participating, with an average gate of ten spectators.

Johnston Technical School football team, April 1911. Photographed in the old Johnston schoolyard which stood at the bottom of South Street. Back row, left to right: A.R. Ramshaw, D.I. Raffles, W. Robinson, E. Alexander, A.W. Atkinson, S.Whalley, P.C. Brown, T. Barr, F.G. Cousins, G. Robinson, P.G. Frogley, W.J. Gibbons Middle row: J. Hudson, H. Bennett, R.H. Ward, G. Ferguson, G. Hauxwell, J. Duke, J. Moreland. Front row: J.H. Hall, W. Davison, A. Addison.

Durham City Rugby Football Club, 1910, winners of the Senior County Cup. Top row, left to right: D. Crampton (Assistant Groundsman), E. Laws (Committee), Col. Turnbull (President), J. Boyd (Hon. Sec. and Treasurer), H.E. Ferens (County Rep.), J. Clark (Groundsman). Middle row: F. Marshall, C. Cranmer, W. Coulson, R. Salvin, J. Turnbull, W. Weavers, W. Cook, R. Bell, D. Elwood, M. Carlin, G. Miller, J. Phillips. Front row: J. Malpass, W. Weighman, H. Imrie, G. Summerscales (Capt.), H. Phillips (Vice-Capt), R. Long, T. Patterson, T. Walker. Taken outside the frontage of the first public swimming baths in Old Elvet.

Gilesgate Rugby Football Club, 1906, taken by John Edis. Top row, left to right: H. Thompson, P.C. Haggie, J. Forrester, A. Reed, B. Milbourne, J. Christie, T. Markham, W. Blagdon,L. Patterson, J.B. Tomlinson, H. Wise, E. Green. Middle row: T. Smith, G. Reed, T. Patterson, H. Alison, W.H. Wood, R.E. Coyne, M. Carling, A. Evison, K. Johnson. Front row: J. Allison, E. Whale, H. Cole, J. Harker, T. Lightfoot, G. Elliot, G. Rowell.

Henderson's Wanderers, Association Football Club, 1902. Henderson's had the carpet factory in the city before Mackay's. Back row, left to right: J. Hortin (Sec.), C. Hortin, W.E. Pounder, H.R. Turnbull, W. Crow, T. Baines (Trainer). Middle row: T. Rowntree, H. Dixon, S. Tulip, C. Matthews, A. Cleminson (Linesman). Front row: R.N. Gibson (Vice-Capt.), R. Williamson (Capt.), R. Bell.

Section Six
WORKING LIFE

Lockey's Supply Stores and Café, 76 Saddler Street, *c.* 1909. The Lockey family were from Rossleigh House, Bede Bank, now the principal's house for the College of St Hild and St Bede. Frank jr, the son of the proprietor, was killed on the Somme in 1916. The family grave is in St Giles' 1870 Cemetery.

A £5 bank note from Jonathan Backhouse & Co., Durham Bank, 1882. Durham Cathedral and Prebends Bridge are illustrated. These notes were hand signed; in this example the signature has been cut out. Jonathan Backhouse & Co. later amalgamated with Barclays Bank.

Plastering gang from Framwellgate, *c.* 1894. Top row, left to right: J. Palmer, J. Plimmer, T. Killian, W. Scott, H. Evans. Front row: A. Pearson, R.A. Pearson, Dick ?, T. Raybole, W. Baker.

George Pescod, dealer in horses, North Road, Durham, *c.* 1900. Durham was once famous for its horse fairs. The fairs faded out in the early 1950s.

Hayton's Novelty Bazaar, Durham Indoor Market, *c.* 1909. Hayton's stall was situated at the left-hand side of the market. The young girls are wearing the fashion of the day with skirts five inches above the ankle. The postcard photograph was sent to Eleanor from Polly, 22 Gilesgate, cancelling a trip to the Palace Theatre. In the top right hand corner can be seen the old market bell.

The staff from Durham City Gas Company, Sidegate, *c.* 1910. The device in the centre of the photograph is for removing water from household gas pipes. Water would build up in the pipes and the lights would flicker and go dim. Some of the names in the group are; Modral, Gibson and Clark.

Fowler's the Grocers, 99 Claypath, *c.* 1914. The shop was established in 1841 by James Fowler, and his son Matthew is seen standing at the entrance. It was in the great miners' strike of 1844 that James Fowler came to the rescue of the Durham miners. He supported them to the best of his ability, and after the strike the miners in return gave him and his business great support. He soon became a man of influence, and was mayor of the city in 1872, 1881–3, 1886 and 1890.

JOHN LOWES & SONS, Monumental Masons and Sculptors,

Photo by Science & Art Co. *Durham.*

Have an exceptionally large stock of ARTIFICIAL WREATHS.

NAT. TEL. 128.

Showrooms—85, CLAYPATH ⎱
Works—180, GILESGATE ⎰ **DURHAM.**

Lowes' Marble Works, *c.* 1908, which stood at the bottom of Gilesgate Bank. In July 1904 Councillor Charles Lowes was killed by one of his apprentices in the building at the rear. He was buried in St Giles' 1870 Cemetery and his grave is marked by a fine, black granite headstone. The apprentice, Robert John Allen, was sentenced to twenty years' imprisonment in Durham Goal. Allen's father was in fact a prison warder at Durham. His girlfriend stood by him and after his release they emigrated to Australia.

Porter's Supply Stores, 43 Gilesgate, which stood to the right of the Drill Hall at the bottom of Gilesgate Bank, *c.* 1947. The manager, Mr Hale, is standing in the doorway. To the right is Station Lane and the back entrance to the 'Volunteer Arms' Hotel. The property was demolished in the 1960s for the new road.

Porter's van at the rear of Porter's, *c.* 1947. Robert Inglis is on the left and on the right is Fred Mulgrew.

Pattison's staff, *c.* 1905. The workforce is seen here outside the workshop behind the Royal County Hotel, Elvet Waterside. The furniture and upholstery business was founded in about 1874 by Mary Pattison. Mary's nephew Arthur Pattison, the large gentleman in the centre of the picture, took over the business. The establishment operated from a retail shop at 16 Elvet Bridge.

Staff from the Durham City Laundry, which was situated near the Sands, *c.* 1925.

The Old Tea Pot was originally outside C.F. White's Wholesale Retailers in the Market Place around 1860. Later the family moved it to Gilesgate post office which stood about 20 yd down from the Old Drill Hall. The photograph shows Miss H. White and her sister Emma Vasey outside Gilesgate post office, *c.* 1899. The tea pot was moved to Fowler's the Grocers, Claypath, then later to the House of Andrews Bookshop, 73 Saddler Street.

A. J. Leeming, M.P.S., CASH CHEMIST and PHARMACIST......

Dispensing Department

All Physicians' Prescriptions are Dispensed at Store Prices with the Purest and Freshest :: Drugs : : : : : Obtainable. : :

All Veterinary Medicines kept in Stock & Prepared according to Private Recipes.

Patent Medicines

at Store Prices.

—:o:—

Toilet Articles, Tooth Brushes, Hair Brushes, Nail Brushes, : Tooth Powders Perfumes, etc.

Everything Stocked which belongs to a Modern Pharmacy.

Photo by Science & Art Co. *Durham*

Leeming's Ivy Leaf Corn Cure, Speedily and Painlessly removes obstinate Corns with two or three applications.

PRICE, 7½D.

STATION CUTTING, NORTH ROAD, DURHAM.

An advertisement for Leeming's Cash Chemist, *c.* 1909, which stood at 57 North Road. The property was demolished in the 1960s to make way for the new road system.

Rolling's the general dealers, 45a Sunderland Road, Gilesgate, *c.* 1949. The building is now a shadow of its former self, a mix of business and student accommodation, with a tarmac frontage.

Mountjoy Hill, showing Elvet Colliery to the left, *c.* 1897 (sunk in 1828). St Oswald's Church can be seen to the right. The church had to be restored in 1834 as a result of mining subsidence from Elvet Colliery. The colliery's main outlet was to local residents. It closed in 1908, mainly because of subterranean flooding and the cost of payments for property which had been damaged by subsidence. Durham University Main Library now occupies the site, opposite the New Inn on the Stockton Road.

Coulson's Boring Contractors from Margery Lane, Crossgate, *c.* 1920. Coulson's was a long established firm in the city and was involved in the opening of the Grange Iron Works at Carrville in 1866. The business in Crossgate continued under Coulson's name for many years.

Gilesgate's first ice-cream shop, 82 Gilesgate, *c.* 1912, which stood next door to the Brewers' Arms. The shop was owned by the Dimambro family who later moved to 90 Claypath. Charlie Dimambro is standing in front of the window.

Staff of Durham County Hospital at the Princess Ballroom in the Three Tuns Hotel. The dinner was held to mark the introduction of the National Health Service Act, 5 July 1948.

The unveiling of the Miners' Memorial at Durham Cathedral, 22 February 1947. The picture includes, left, Tommy Daniels, middle, Harry Inglis and right, Robert Scott from Bearpark Colliery. The memorial is in black Spanish mahogany and was designed by Donald McIntyre. Originally it was a fireplace in Ramside Hall, Carrville, to the east of the city and was given by the Pemberton family.

Three lamp boys from Sherburn Colliery, c. 1910. The postcard had the name Blacklock on the reverse and the address, 24 Dragon Villa, Sherburn Road. The average age of lamp boys was fourteen.

Men working on the old A1 road near Farewell Hall, *c.* 1938. This group was very fortunate to have work, as it was scarce in Durham in the 1920s; soup kitchens were operating for those in need.

The building of Durham School Chapel, 1926. The chapel was built as a memorial to Dunelmians who had been killed in the First World War and was dedicated on 30 September 1926. A former pupil, killed on the first day of the Somme campaign, 1 July 1916, was the poet William Noel Hodgson of the 9th Devonshire Regiment. He had attended the school from 1905 to 1911. The chapel's architect and designer was Mr Brierley of Messrs Brierley and Rutherford of York. The contract work was carried out by Messrs Rudd and Son of Grantham.

Section Seven
THE BUILT ENVIRONMENT

Bakehouse Lane, Gilesgate, c. 1933. This lane marked the boundary of St Giles' parish. To the right is what was the General Gordon public house, 63 Claypath. The lane became known as Kepier Terrace and reverted to Bakehouse Lane in recent times. The lane originally led to the communal bakehouse.

Sherburn Road Ends, *c.* 1904, taken by John Edis. To the right is the Queen's Head public house and on the left is what was known locally as the Store Corner. The property on the left stood on an ancient site known as the Maidens Bower. St Giles' Church records of 1629 show various entries for repairs to the Maidens Bower, which was described in 1860 as 'an enclosure used by the servant maids of Durham for milking their cows'.

The Duckpond, Gilesgate, *c.* 1947. The earliest reference to the Duckpond is 1584, when Rycharde Robinson was paid for scouring the Ducke Poole. The public health report of 1849 advises that the Duckpond be filled in and a water trough placed nearby for animals. A water trough still survives at the top of Gilesgate Bank.

Gilesgate Bank, *c.* 1910, looking towards the city. A 'dry bridge' can be seen in the centre; this was removed in 1923. Most of the property was demolished in the 1960s.

Woodbine Cottage which stood near Baths Bridge. On the left is the exit of Tinklers Lane (St Giles' parish boundary). The small sweet-shop can be seen at the bottom of the lane. Woodbine Cottage was a Georgian building that had to be demolished because of a landslide from the new Leazes Road. This photograph shows the occupants leaving on a cold November day in 1965.

Looking down Ravensworth Terrace, Gilesgate, c. 1946. The buildings on the left were removed to make way for the new Leazes Road.

Kepier Mill, gatehouse and the manor house of the Heaths, *c.* 1880. The mill was destroyed by fire on 24 September 1870 when the miller's son fell asleep and forgot to fill the hopper with corn. The gatehouse was built by Bishop Richard de Bury (1333–45). The manor house of the Heaths was built in the late sixteenth century. The house later became the White Bear Inn and in its final years the Kepier Inn; sadly it was demolished in 1892.

The restoration of Prebends' Bridge, Durham City, *c.* 1955. The earlier bridge was swept away in the great flood of 1771. The present bridge was built by George Nicholson, the cathedral mason, and was started in 1772.

Prebends' Cottage, which stands on the south side of Prebends' Bridge, *c.* 1900. The cottage has changed very little over the last hundred years; it is the property of the dean and chapter.

Looking down New Elvet, *c.* 1900. The spire in the centre is that of the United Reformed Church (now redundant), Claypath. The Hare and Hounds Hotel stands five properties down from the left. All of the property in this picture was demolished to make way for Durham University's Elvet Riverside and Dunelm House. Small retail shops now occupy the right-hand side.

The first Baths Bridge, *c.* 1875. It was built in 1855 by public subscription, organized by Mr Edward Peele, who had a veterinary business in the city. The bridge provided a convenient crossing, linking Elvet to Gilesgate. The wooden bridge was replaced in 1896 by the iron bridge, which in turn was removed in 1962.

The removal in 1962 of the second Baths Bridge, built in 1896 at a cost of £700. The public baths stand to the right. The new concrete structure is very similar to the first bridge of 1855.

South side of St Giles' Church, *c*. 1830, drawn by William Pearson. The south aisle was added during the restoration of the church, 1873–6. In May 1894, while workmen were laying the new chancel floor, the vault was opened and examined. A number of coffins were found, belonging to the Heath family of Kepier. The vault was measured and resealed.

St Giles' Church from the lane which leads to Pelaw Wood, *c*. 1947. In March 1916 a poem about the ghost of St Giles' Churchyard appeared in the Durham Advertiser. The ghost was reputed to have been seen travelling down this lane in the direction of the ancient Holy Well which stood near the Silver Link Footbridge in Pelaw Wood.

Durham Observatory, *c.* 1840. The building was designed by Salvin and erected around 1840 by private subscription. An observer lived in the purpose-built house and worked under the direction of the Revd Temple Chevallier. In the first volume of his History of Durham, published in 1860, Fordyce records that Durham had the only established astronomical observatory between London and Edinburgh.

The obelisk which stands 100 ft high near Obelisk Lane, Western Hill, in the grounds of St Leonard's School, c. 1969. The obelisk was erected by W.L. Wharton of Dryburn Hall in 1850 at his own expense. He gave it to the observatory to use as a landmark to sight the observatory telescope. It marks the meridian 1,200 yd north.

The statue of the 3rd Marquess of Londonderry in Hussars uniform, *c.* 1925. This fine electroplated statue was unveiled on 2 December 1861. The sculptor was Raffaelle Monti (1818–81), a Milanese who came to England in 1848 and lived here until his death. This statue is considered to be his finest work. To the left of the statue is the city fire ladder and the railings belonging to the gents' underground toilets.

Kingsgate Bridge, looking towards Elvet, 1963, taken by George Lye. The bridge was designed by the late Sir Ove Arup and was opened in December 1963. The £36,000 bridge was commissioned by Durham University to provide a route across the river from Elvet to the peninsula. Its design and construction provided a talking-point; two slender V-shaped supports and decks were built on rotating bases on opposite banks of the river and then swung round to meet in the middle, 60 ft above the water. In December 1993, thirty years after its construction, it was awarded a Mature Concrete Structure Award by the Concrete Society for its timeless quality and elegant design.

This photograph is a testimony to the days when winters were white. It was taken outside the Woodman Inn, Lower Gilesgate, in 1938, taken by Danny Webster. The snow-plough is fighting its way through a blizzard.

Property at the bottom of Gilesgate Bank, *c.* 1966, demolished in about 1967 to make way for the new roundabout. The Drill Hall can be seen in the centre. It was here in August 1904 that General William Booth, the Salvation Army leader, gave a public lecture to the people of Durham.

Gilesgate Church of England School, 1966. The school was opened in October 1874; it later became the Parish Hall and Sunday School. During the last war it was used as a first-aid post. In its later years it became neglected and was demolished to make way for St Giles' Filling Station.

Gilesgate Moor, 1929, taken by John Edis. The Rex Cinema stands to the centre right of the picture. This was opened in 1930 by local grocer George Lamb. Before the local Catholic church was built it was used on Sundays for mass.

Elvet Bridge, *c.* 1900, taken by Fred Morgan, showing the Paradise Lane area behind the present-day boat house. The chimney in the centre is that of Chisman's Iron and Brass Foundry.

Ivy Cottage, which stood near Brown's Boat House at the bottom of Paradise Lane, *c.* 1921. Because of its location it was often subjected to flood damage; it was also reputed to have had a ghost. The house was demolished in the 1960s to make way for the new road system and for the new Elvet Bridge.

A romantic view of Kepier from the Gilesgate goods line, *c.* 1933. The fields in the background are now part of Newton Hall Housing Estate which, when built in the '70s, was believed to be the largest private housing estate in Europe.

Steps leading to the gatehouse at Kepier, *c.* 1930. The old mangle is a reminder of the days when washing was an all-day chore which involved younger members of the family turning the handle on the mangle as the mother fed the washing through the rollers.

Shacklock Hall, *c.* 1840, home of the Henderson family who owned the carpet factory at Freemans Place. This house had previously been a farm and stood near the factory. The incident in the engraving is from William Henderson's *Notes and Reminiscences of My Life as an Angler* (1876), and involves the family cat.

North Road, *c.* 1900. It was constructed in 1831 to improve the Great North Road. Before this date the main route to the north was the old street of Framwellgate. The domed tower on the right belonged to the old Miner's Hall which was officially opened in 1876.

The Market Place in 1830, showing the old St Nicholas' Church, which was taken down in June 1857. Standing to the left of the church is the town house of the Nevilles; this was replaced by the new town hall, built in 1850 and officially opened on 29 January 1851.

St Nicholas' Church, Durham City, c. 1978. The church was refurbished in 1980 by the vicar, the Revd Dr George Carey, now Archbishop of Canterbury. It was rededicated by the Bishop of Durham on 23 October 1981.

An old cottage, then lived in by the parish clerk of St Gile's Church, *c.* 1900, which stood two doors up from the Britannia Inn. This building is typical of the style associated with Durham City. Many properties like this were demolished in the 1920s and 1930s. The dormer windows, pantile roofs and stone tiles were very common; now only a handful survive.

Count's House, *c.* 1890. This was in fact a summerhouse (listed in 1857 as Shipperdon's Cottage) belonging to a house in the South Bailey. It is commonly called the Count's House after the Polish Count Boruwlaski who lodged at the home of the Ebdons near Prebends' Bridge.

Looking towards the Old Elm Tree public house, 12 Crossgate, *c.* 1928. The property to the right of the Elm Tree was replaced with council flats in the 1960s (Grape Lane).

Market Place Mill, *c.* 1933. Durham Ice Rink now stands to the left of the photograph. The mill was commonly called Martin's Flour Mill after the owner.

Section Eight
MILITARY MATTERS

Buglers of the 1st Battalion Durham Light Infantry playing on the balcony of the town hall in July 1960. The battalion had been involved in a recruiting campaign.

Soldiers from the 43rd North Durham Militia in undress uniform on the steps of Durham Castle, *c.* 1865. The local gentry acted as officers while volunteers for the rank and file had to be drawn by ballot. The main role of the militia was home defence and in a time of war they could take over coastal defences, thereby releasing regular soldiers for services overseas.

The Militia Barracks (Vane-Tempest Hall), *c.* 1947, as drawn by Norman Richley, who was curate at St Giles' Church. In April 1864 contracts were given for the building of the barracks: Mr R. Alan, mason; Mr Appleby (Barnard Castle), joiner; Mr Pearson, joiner; and Mr P. Rules, slater. The building was opened in 1865 for the 43rd North Durham Militia. By the early 1880s the building was empty. The city took over the barracks in 1884 and used them as a smallpox hospital. In 1892 the barracks were purchased by Lord Londonderry for the 2nd Durham Artillery Volunteers. Until the late '30s many military occupants passed through. In the last war the tower was used as a look-out post for the ARP wardens. It was here that the idea came to light for a community building. The Gilesgate Welfare Association was formed in 1947.

The 8th Durham Light Infantry Headquarters, *c.* 1966. The building was officially opened 7 February 1902. The Drill Hall stood at the bottom of Gilesgate Bank near the site of the roundabout; it had to be demolished to make way for the new through road in 1967. The coat of arms above the entrance was saved and is now incorporated in the new Drill Hall building (TA Centre).

Men from the 2nd Durham Volunteer Artillery, who were based at the barracks (Vane-Tempest Hall), *c.* 1905. Richard Savage is to the left in the front row. Many of these men would have been from the city area, as the volunteers were weekend soldiers.

Private Alfred Savage (brother of Richard, above, and Jack, opposite), seen here, in 1912, proudly wearing his uniform of the 8th Durhams. Alf later went on to join the Royal Field Artillery in 1913. He was one of the first to be called to the front in August 1914.

Private Jack Savage from Gilesgate, *c.* 1916.
Jack was in the Royal Field Artillery in the
First World War. After the war Jack was never
the same. The British Army expected men to
come home and to get on with life, but the
war had affected Jack badly. A page from his
sister's diary records that he left home on 25
August 1922. Jack was never to be seen again
by his family in Durham.

The band of the 8th Durhams, *c.* 1927. The original photograph is entitled 'Boys of the Old Brigade'.
Back row, far right, is Herbert Richardson whose father was head gardener at St Hild's College. They
lived in School House, which was attached to the college.

Territorials from the 8th Durhams leaving the Market Place for Palace Green, Coronation Day, 22 June 1911. The coronation of George V was a great occasion for the city; all the streets and premises were ablaze with flags and floral decorations.

The Boer War memorial, 24 October 1912. The occasion was the laying of the colours of the 1st, 2nd and 3rd Battalions Durham Light Infantry. The cross was erected in December 1905 in memory of the men of the Durham Light Infantry who had lost their lives in the South African War. The cross was designed by Mr C.G. Hodges of Hexham and sculpted by Mr G.W. Milburn of York.

Durham Officer Training Corps Contingent, Hatfield Hall, 3 May 1913. The procession is seen here walking to the main entrance from the main gates in the North Bailey. The occasion was the installation of the new chancellor, the Duke of Northumberland, His Grace Henry George Percy KG. In the procession is the Prime Minister, Herbert Henry Asquith, the Bishop of London and Earl Curzon.

3rd Northumbrian Brigade, Royal Field Artillery, Durham City Battery, 1914. The scene is Durham Market Place, and they were about to leave for France. Most of the men were recruited from the city and were based at the barracks in Gilesgate.

A group of servicemen in the garden of Ivy Cottage, which stood near Brown's Boat House, *c.* 1915, taken by George Fillingham. In the centre are Mr Joseph Pattison (without hat), his wife Janet and children, Thomas and Mary.

The Curtis family, 13 Claypath, c. 1916. Mrs Curtis is wearing a Northumberland Fusiliers shoulder badge and her son on the far right wears a cap badge in his lapel. The man of the household, Charles Curtis, was fighting in France. This type of photograph was common as copies would be sent to loved ones at the front. Back row, left to right: Alice, Mary, Elizabeth (mother), Elsie, William and Charles. Front row: Elizabeth and Emma.

Durham City heroes, June 1917, taken by George Fillingham. Left to right: Pte. Mathew Hanley DLI, awarded the Military Medal for bravery on the Somme after carrying six wounded men to safety under heavy shell fire; Sgt. W.H. Smith DLI, awarded Military Medal for saving two comrades who were wounded and under heavy shell fire; L/Cpl. Richard Savage, 10th Royal Hussars, awarded the Distinguished Conduct Medal in October 1914, for saving two officers under heavy shell and rifle fire who were lying wounded in no man's land. The naval officer in the front row is unknown. The framed illuminated addresses were presented by the Mayor of Durham.

Anniversary Memorial Service, 1925. The anniversary was to commemmorate the first action at Grafenstafel Ridge during the Second Battle of Ypres in April 1915. The venue was the old Militia Barracks (now Vane-Tempest Hall), Gilesgate. Back row, left to right: Lieut. J. Bramwell, Lieut. Watson, Captain J.N.O. Rogers, Lieut. S. Platten MC, Captain T.A. Saint, Captain J.R. MacDonald MC, RAMC, Lieut. S. Aberdeen DCM, Lieut. Willis. Middle row: Captain J. Hornsby, Lieut. A. Rooney, MC, Lieut. Eltringham, Captain Harmer, Col. C. Lomax CF, Captain T.A. Bradford DSO, Captain G.E. Blackett, Captain J. Atkinson DCM, Captain T.F. Brass, Lieut. J.G. Raine MC, Captain H. Wilkinson MC, T.D, Lieut. Alderson, Lieut. E. Fisher. Front row: Captain E.A. Leybourne TD, Major E.H. Veitch MC, TD, Major J.A.S. Ritson DSO, MC, TD, Major J. Turnbull, TD, Colonel J. Turnbull, CMG, VD, Lieut.-Col. J.R. Ritson OBE, TD, Colonel W.C. Blackett CBE, TD, Captain H.A. Stenhouse, Captain W. Francis, Captain E.H. Motum, Captain R.A. Worswick.

The Northumberland Hussars, B Squadron (Territorials), 1928. The Hussars were a cavalry unit based at the barracks. Most of the men were local lads who joined to have some excitement at weekends. One regular exercise was tent-pegging; this was when mounted Hussars armed with lances would try to retrieve tent-pegs from the ground. Standing second from the right is Ambrose Savage (the author's great uncle).

St Cuthbert's Church Lads' Brigade, c. 1928. Back row, left to right: Billy Palmer, Henry Gibson, John Lee, Robbie Peel. Front row: Walter Robinson and Ronnie Modral. The brigade was run by Cecil Ferens, a solicitor, from Saddler Street.

An historic visit to Durham by the 1st Battalion, Durham Light Infantry, on Saturday 21 July 1934. The photograph was taken at Sherburn Road Ends, Gilesgate. The title of the photograph was 'Three cheers to the Mayor' (Councillor J.C. Fowler). After a short speech by the mayor they were entertained at the barracks (Vane Tempest Hall).

St Giles' knitting circle at the vicarage *c.* 1939, knitting for the troops. The photograph shows the strong community spirit that was built up in the early days of the Second World War.

Mrs Pragnell from Claypath, seen here collecting her ration of coal in 1943. This scene was quite common in the north of England until the 1950s. Coal delivery dates were an opportunity for youngsters to earn a penny or two for carrying the coal to their neighbours' coalhouses. The spire is that of the United Reformed Church (now redundant).

Durham City Auxiliary Fire Brigade, pictured down on The Sands at the bottom of Providence Row, 1940. The brigade was stationed nearby. The large chimney was from Sidegate brickworks and the house belonged to the sewage works on the opposite side of the river.

Durham Auxiliary Fire Service, September 1940. Allergate station members are about to take part in a practice at Durham City Baths. The section officer in charge was Mr J. Dunn. Durham had the first ladies' crew in the north of England. In the background to the right is Woodbine Cottage.

The Post Office Home Guard Platoon, *c.* 1942. The photograph was taken at the rear of the old post office in Claypath. Exercises were held at Kepier Rifle Range; the platoon's arms consisted of one Thompson machine-gun and one .303 rifle. Back row, left to right: Ross Cunningham, -?-, -?-, A. Dunn, F. King, -?-, -?-, S. Jordan, H. Winter, -?-, T. Hardy. Middle row: H. Marley, F. Bateman, H. Mole, A. Lawson, H. Harris, N. Alison, J.F. Magee, G.A. Johnson, T. Herbert, P. Hart, D. Cook, H. McGregor. Frontrow: J. McClurg, S. Grant, G. Thompson, F. Spirit, C. Donaldson, T. Blythe, J. Ward, F. Benson, J. Wilson.

Durham City Air Training Corps, *c.* 1941. In the front row behind the cross is Ron Liddle from Pittington and behind him is Cecil Ferens, who was commanding officer. Meetings were held at Whinney Hill School. Many of the men went on to join the Royal Air Force.

Section Nine
TRANSPORT

London & North Eastern Railway bus service operating from Durham railway station, *c.* 1930. The bus is a Birmingham-built SOS 'S' type, normal control, 31-seater, bought by Northern General Transport in 1926.

Elvet station, *c.* 1948 (opened in 1893), which stood on the site now occupied by the Magistrates' Court. The station was the terminus of a short branch line which ran through Sherburn where it joined two other spurs, one to Whitwell Colliery and the other to Shincliffe. The station was closed to passengers in January 1931, but continued to carry Miners' Gala passengers each July until 1953. Between 1931 and 1949 it was used as a goods station. The station was sold to Durham County Council in 1949 and demolished in 1963.

An engine leaving Elvet station, *c.* 1949. Sherburn Road Estate can be seen on the left.

London & North Eastern Railway engine (LNER/BR Class 'J39' 0–6–0 locomotive) leaving the turntable at Elvet station, *c.* 1949, after working a Miners' Gala special. On the right is the water-tower used for filling the engines.

Horse-drawn prison van outside Durham railway station, 1906, taken by W. Wilkinson. Many older residents remember waiting for the 'Black Maria' to come down from the station with the policeman riding on the back.

Gilesgate goods station as seen from the old Engine Bridge, 1966. This was the first passenger station in the city and had opened in June 1844. The goods station was closed on 7 November 1966 under the Beeching plan. Beyond, to the right of this picture, was Kipling's coal yard.

Durham station including the engine sheds, *c.* 1958. The area is now a large car park for the station.

Belmont Viaduct, which linked Belmont to Brasside, c. 1933. This viaduct had been opened in 1856. It was one of the loftiest bridges of its kind in the kingdom. It stretched across the Wear at a height of 130 ft. The piers stand on stone which was brought from the Roman quarry at Rudchester, Northumberland.

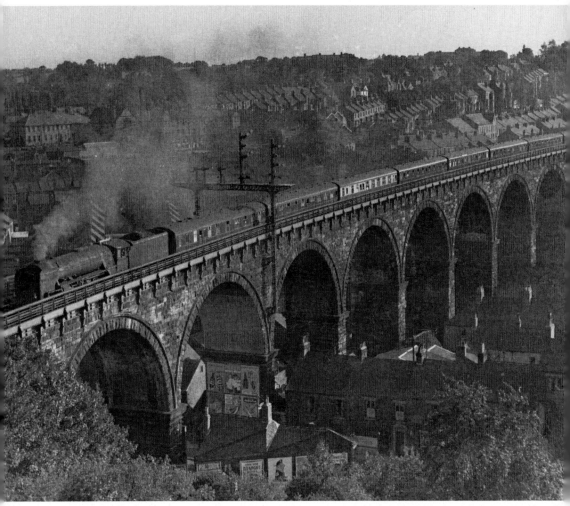

Durham Viaduct in the 1950s. Designed by the North Eastern Railway contractor Mr R. Cail, the viaduct had opened in 1857. It is 832 ft long and nearly 100 ft high, and has eleven arches. During its construction there were great problems with the foundations; long oak piles were driven by steam-power through peat moss and quicksand. The spaces between the piles were then filled with concrete; all together 21,300 ft of piling was used, as well as 184,500 cu ft of ashlar, 56,000 cu ft of brickwork, 140,000 cu ft of rubble and 142,000 cu ft of dry filling.

Mr J.W. Blackburn, 50 Dragon Villa, Sherburn Road, *c.* 1892. The cart was specially designed to transport Anglo-American lamp oil.

Blackburn's Cab Hire from Dragon Villa outside Woodlands and Caselaw on Gilesgate Green, *c.* 1900.

Durham bus station, *c.* 1958. St Godric's Church stands proudly in the background. The station was completed in 1929 on the site of what was R.V. Hill's flour mill. The old station was taken down in the 1970s and part of it is now at Beamish Open Air Museum, awaiting re-erection.

Express bus which operated from the Market Place to Murton, *c.* 1927. The Express Service Omnibus Company was started by Mr William Showler in the early 1920s. The depot was at Gilesgate Moor opposite the Travellers' Rest public house.

The chief constable's car, a Daimler 10 hp, *c.* 1929, at the rear of the old police station, Elvet, taken by John Edis.

Temporary Police Constable Fred Forbes (left), *c.* 1928. Fred was from Whinney Hill and started as a TPC in 1926 during the General Strike. He worked with Durham Police Force until retirement in 1960. The van shown here was the new motorized 'Black Maria' used to transport prisoners. The body was built by Fred Forbes on a Lancia chassis.

Wood & Watson's wagon fleet, *c.* 1936. This photograph was taken in the barracks field, now Wood & Watson's car park. The wagons advertise a new drink, Watcheer. Wood and Watson's, 132 Gilesgate, are Durham's longest surviving mineral water manufacturers, established in about 1890. The founder, William Henry Wood, was mayor of the city in 1909 and 1919. He had come to Durham from Bedlington Colliery, Northumberland, where his family owned Wood & Sons Ltd, mineral water manufacturers. Initially he had premises near the County Hospital, before moving to Gilesgate around 1894. The first trade mark of the factory was 'seven embossed stars', shortly after, it changed to the towers of Durham Cathedral. Their stone ginger-beer bottles are now very rare and are collectors' items.

Silver Street at its narrowest point, *c.* 1965. Until 1967 this road was the main route through the city centre. The bus is a United Bristol 'LS' type, servicing Durham to Peterlee.

A lucky escape for the driver of this car, which was sandwiched between two buses on Gilesgate Bank, *c.* 1968.

Arthur Nesbitt's van on Palace Green outside Cosins Hall, 1953. Arthur Nesbitt ran a radio and television service on Elvet Bridge opposite Magdalene Steps.

Traffic congestion, Elvet Bridge, c. 1970. The bridge was restricted to pedestrians only in the mid 1970s.

Durham's first police box, *c.* 1955, used for directing traffic through the Market Place. This was the first of its kind in the country. The man in the box is said to be PC Tommy Stephenson.

The naming of the Durham Light Infantry steam engine, April 1958. The ceremony took place at Durham station in the presence of Mr T.H. Summerson, chairman of British Rail, and Col. K.M. Leather, who commanded the Light Infantry brigade.

Acknowledgements

So many people have donated photographs to the Gilesgate Archive that it is impossible to thank them individually. Institutions which have helped include:

Durham University Library, Palace Green • Durham City Reference Library
Durham Arts, Libraries & Museums Department, Durham County Council
the Taylor Collection • the Armstrong Trust • the trustees of the
Durham Light Infantry Museum

Without this assistance this book would never have been possible and the author acknowledges it gratefully. If any reader has new material or information, it would be helpful if contact was made with: Mr Michael Richardson, 128 Gilesgate, Durham DH1 1QG (0191-384-1427). Email: gilesgatearchive@aol.com